HOW THEY MADE THINGS WORK!
IN THE AGE OF INDUSTRY

Written by Richard Platt • Illustrated by David Lawrence

W
FRANKLIN WATTS
LONDON•SYDNEY

Published in 2018 by The Watts Publishing Group

Text copyright © Richard Platt 2010
Illustrations copyright © Franklin Watts 2010

Editor in Chief John C. Miles
Art Director Jonathan Hair
Design/Additional artworks Matthew Lilly
Editor Sarah Ridley
Picture researcher Sarah Smithies The right of Richard Platt to
be identified as the author of the work has been asserted by him in
accordance with the Copyright, Designs and Patents Act 1988.

Picture credits: Mary Evans P. L.: back cover, 19. The Granger Collection/
TopFoto: 17l, 25b. Hulton Archive / Getty Images: 26. National Railway
Museum / Science & Society P.L:7. Oxford Science Archive / HIP /
TopFoto: 12, 15. Private Collection / The Bridgeman Art Library: 22. Ann
Ronan Picture Library / HIP / TopFoto: 28. Science Museum / Science
& Society Picture Library: 13, 17r. Topfoto: 23, 24, 25t. Universal Images
Group Limited / Alamy: 27. CC Wikimedia Commons: 16. World History
Archive / TopFoto: 9, 29t.

Every attempt has been made to clear copyright. Should there be any
inadvertent omission please apply to the publisher for rectification.

A CIP catalogue record is available from the British Library.

Dewey number: 609

ISBN 978 14451 6431 1

Printed in China

Franklin Watts
An imprint of
Hachette Children's Group
Part of the Watts Publishing Group
Carmelite House
50 Victoria Embankment
London EC4Y 0DZ

An Hachette UK Company
www.hachette.co.uk
www.franklinwatts.co.uk

Contents

HOW THEY MADE THINGS WORK IN THE AGE OF INDUSTRY

Nicknamed "the Age of Industry", the 19th century was when the modern world itself was invented. When the century began, horses were the fastest way to get around; when it finished, motor cars raced them on the roads. In 1800, communication meant waving a flag; by 1900 radio messages flashed news instantly.

At the start of the century, a boat race or a piece of music were pleasures that lasted a moment; at the end they could be preserved forever and replayed over and over again.

A gramophone at a late-Victorian dance (see pages 18–19).

Progress

Some of the changes in technology started the century before. Traditionally, everything had been made by hand with the simplest of tools. But in the 18th century machines grew in importance. They made goods more quickly and more cheaply. To tend and feed the machines, labourers moved from small home workshops into huge, noisy factories. To keep the machines turning and the workers at their weary tasks, there was a new source of power. Hissing and hot, steam was quickly replacing the wind, water and animals that had kept things moving in the past.

Inventors

Nineteenth-century inventors were different, too. In previous ages, two kinds of people made discoveries and improvements. Craftsmen such as blacksmiths used their intelligence and strength to make things work in new ways. Wealthy gentlemen thought up scientific ideas to devise better mechanisms. But with the spread of education, a new profession appeared: the engineer. Engineers were neither oily mechanics, nor gentleman dabblers. They were practical scientists. With knowledge and ingenuity, they turned bright ideas into machines that changed the world. Some, such as Thomas Edison, became as famous as some rock stars are today.

Thomas Edison and his light bulb (see pages 10-11).

STEAM RAILWAYS

In the distance, a plume of smoke rises. A deep panting sound grows gradually louder, until it finally appears: a shiny steam train, and travelling at the terrifying speed of 50 kilometres (km) an hour (30 mph)!

Steam trains carried Victorian people faster and farther than ever before. They transformed Britain, changing where everyone lived, how they worked and relaxed, and even what they ate.

Snorting monsters! That's what they are!

Can't you go any faster?

Getting about was soooo slowww before the train. The 320-km (200-mile) journey from London to Manchester took a horse-drawn carriage more than four days in 1750. In winter the muddy roads could double this time. Horses also pulled the heaviest goods in barges, on a newly-built network of canals. This was even slower than travelling by road.

Can't stop, we're in a hurry!

Canal barges could carry far more than carts, and they never got stuck in the mud, but they were still slow.

Steaming along

British mining companies first used steam engines to pump water in the 18th century. They also built roads of metal rails to stop the horse-drawn wagons from getting bogged down in mud. In 1804, Cornish engineer Richard Trevithick fitted wheels to a steam engine, and created a locomotive that ran on rails. Within 20 years railway companies were using locomotives to pull passengers and freight. They proved that rail travel was fast and cheap. A web of rail lines quickly spread across Europe.

Fresh food & fun

Steam trains rushed to markets foods that rotted easily, and gave many city-dwellers their first taste of fresh milk. Low fares made it possible for working people to take holidays, and seaside resorts, such as Blackpool or Cleethorpes, boomed.

The winner of a famous 1829 locomotive competition, the Rainhill Trials, was George and Robert Stephenson's Rocket. Locomotives used the same basic design for the next 130 years.

Locomotives were such a novelty that a huge crowd gathered at Rainhill to watch them race.

How locomotives worked

Heated by a coal fire, water inside a boiler turned to steam. This pressed on a piston, forcing it back and forth inside a strong tube. The piston's movement drove round the locomotive's wheels.

boiler

cylinder contains piston

Not everyone loved locomotives. One writer called them, "monsters navigated by a tail of smoke".

IRON SHIPS

What will they think of next?

When the 19th century began, a sea voyage was an exciting adventure, but it could be uncomfortable and perhaps dangerous as well. Ships were made of wood and powered by wind. Cabins were tiny and the food was terrible. Steel ships and steam power transformed travel. But by the end of the century, wealthy travellers might not guess they were at sea: passenger liners were huge and luxurious.

Why aren't we moving?

Sailing had always been the fastest, and often the only, way to travel long distances. But when the wind didn't blow, sailing ships simply didn't sail. Their wooden hulls were another problem. Wood wasn't strong enough to build really big ships, and even small ones needed a lot of timber to withstand huge ocean waves. Ships' hulls could be 60 cm (2 ft) thick.

You can't be Sirius?

Few believed steamships would succeed because the fuel they needed would fill the cargo hold. They were almost right. The crew of the first steamship to cross the Atlantic non-stop, the *Sirius*, in 1838, had to burn the furniture when the coal ran out!

At this rate we'll only clear the harbour by Christmas!

Because sailing depended on the weather, no ships sailed to a regular timetable until 1818.

8

Full steam ahead!

Until the late 18th century, it was impossible to make iron plates big or strong enough to build a ship. But improvements in metalworking transformed travel. By 1800, shipbuilders were making hulls from 6 cm (2.5 in) of iron instead of ten times this thickness of timber. Steam engines first powered small ships in 1807, when American inventor Robert Fulton used one to drive a small river boat. Modern ocean-going steamships began in 1845 when the gigantic *Great Britain* crossed the Atlantic.

Costly crossing

The cheapest ticket to New York on *Great Britain* cost 20 guineas: five month's wages for the workers who built it.

At nearly 100 m (325 ft) in length, Isambard Kingdom Brunel's Great Britain was the world's biggest ship by far when launched in 1843. It was the first to combine an iron hull with a steam-driven propeller.

Brunel's a genius!

The Great Britain could carry up to 360 passengers from Bristol to New York in two weeks.

Brunel's Great Eastern became the world's biggest ship when launched in 1858. It kept the record for 41 years.

Bigger is better!

Isambard Kingdom Brunel built his steamships as big as he could after he had a brilliant but simple idea. He worked out that a huge ship would burn four times as much coal as one half its size, but could carry eight times more cargo or passengers. So the bigger the ship, the less it would cost to run.

LIGHT BULB

I see the light!

Imagine a world where most activity stops when the sun goes down. Flickering flames cast small puddles of dim yellow light indoors. People travelling at night wait for a full moon so they can see their way. This was the world before the electric light bulb: an extraordinary invention that literally turned night into day.

You'll ruin your eyes in this light!

Candles, oil and gas lamps were only just bright enough to read and sew by, and needed careful attention, otherwise they could set light to clothes or furnishings.

Flaming night-lights

After dark, there was only one way to light a room: burn something! Candles and oil lamps were traditional sources of light. However, they were not very bright, and needed regular refilling or replacement. From about 1820, gas was piped along city streets, and those who could afford a supply lit their homes with gas jets.

Light up the petrel

Anything oily can stand in for a candle: until the late-19th century the people of Britain's Shetland islands caught and killed thousands of greasy stormy petrel seabirds. Threaded with wicks and burned, the feathered corpses lit the long winter nights.

Let there be light

Early electricity experimenters noticed around 1800 that electric power heated thin wires until they glowed white. However, gas lights were brighter, and the wires soon burned out. Over the next 80 years more than 20 inventors tried to make brighter, longer-lasting electric lights. American Thomas Edison had the most success. He replaced the hot wire with a strip of charred bamboo, enclosed it in a glass globe and sucked out the air. His "electric lamp" glowed for 1,200 hours before it needed replacing.

Edison spent many frustrating months of research before he perfected the glowing filament of his bulb (left). When asked if he had failed, he replied, "I have not failed. I have just found 10,000 ways that do not work."

American enterprise!

Edison showed off his "thousand light" generator, the world's biggest, in October 1881.

Supplying the system

Thomas Edison's light bulb succeeded because he realised that the bulb was just one part of a much larger electric system. As well as bulbs, he sold sockets to hold them, switches and meters. He built dynamos to generate electric power, and laid cables to distribute it to homes and offices.

TELEGRAPH

On a windy hilltop, wooden arms flap lazily at the top of a tall tower. In the far distance, an identical tower exactly copies the sequence of movements. It's 1847, and this semaphore telegraph is the latest thing in communication. It takes half an hour to send a short message and in just a year it will be replaced by a far better telegraph, powered by electricity.

This new telegraph seems 'armless to me!

Arms and towers

Since the earliest times, people have used hilltop fires to send yes-or-no messages. Around 1790 French inventor Claude Chappe devised something better: a waving arm telegraph that spelled out whole words. Chappe's system soon covered all of France, and other countries copied it. However, it needed towers 10 km (6 miles) apart, teams of trained operators — and fog stopped all messages.

Are... you... coming... home... for... lunch?

Inside a telegraph tower, one operator used a telescope to watch the next tower. He called out the arm positions to another operator, who copied them using handles that moved the arms atop the tower. At the destination, a translator looked up the signals in a code book, which listed the meaning of each combination of arm positions.

Dot-dashy-dot-dot-dash

Expert telegraph clerks could tap out 20 words a minute on the keys.

American professor Joseph Henry showed in 1831 that electricity in a wire could ring a bell a mile away. Within six years several inventors devised electric telegraph systems. The most successful was named after American artist and inventor Samuel Morse who devised it, with much technical help. Morse telegraph operators tapped messages on a special switch, which sent short and long bursts of electricity down a wire. The pulses powered a "sounder" at the other end. Skilled operators listening to its "click-clack" sound could receive messages at 60 words a minute.

The first electric telegraph lines were strung on poles alongside railways, and the messages were used to control the trains.

Morse key

Telegraph operators tapped out messages on a switch called a Morse key (right). They tapped a code of dots (short taps) and dashes (long ones) to represent each letter of the alphabet. The most common letters in English had the shortest codes, to speed up sending.

Phone, don't tap

When the telephone was invented in 1875, a web of telegraph lines already criss-crossed the world. Telephones thus had a ready-made network of wires over which to send voice calls.

Morse code			
A	•~	N	~•
B	~•••	O	~~~
C	~•~•	P	•~~•
D	~••	Q	~~•~
E	•	R	•~•
F	••~•	S	•••
G	~~•	T	~
H	••••	U	••~
I	••	V	•••~
J	•~~~	W	•~~
K	~•~	X	~••~
L	•~••	Y	~•~~
M	~~	Z	~~••

PHOTOGRAPHY

"I've been framed!"

"From today, painting is dead!" With these words, a French artist greeted the first photographs, taken by French showman Louis Daguerre in 1839. Daguerre's pictures were truly astonishing. They recorded even the tiniest details on highly-polished silver plates. Those who saw them called them "mirrors with memories". Photography didn't put painters out of work but it made worthless their ability to copy reality onto canvas.

Palette, canvas and easel

Until Daguerre's invention, the only way to record the world was with a brush or pencil. Artists spent years studying, and more years practising their skills before they could earn a living. Portrait and landscape paintings were not too difficult, but painters just had to guess what fast-moving subjects looked like.

"How long will this take?"

"If you sit still, about 16 weeks."

Painting a portrait might take several weeks. The subject had to return to the artist's studio many times, and sit in just the same position.

Metal clamps and stands made sure that portrait subjects kept absolutely still.

Clamped and ready

Daguerre coated copper plates in silver, and made them sensitive to light with fumes of the chemical iodine. Projecting onto the plate an image from a lens created a latent (invisible) picture. The vapour of a liquid metal, mercury, revealed the image. Taking the picture took half a minute: anything that moved in that time looked blurred.

Kept in the dark

For nearly 40 years, taking pictures needed almost as much skill as painting. Photographers messed around with smelly, poisonous chemicals. They needed dimly-lit "darkrooms" to prepare plates and process pictures. And photography was no better than paint at catching movement. But in 1878 the "dry plate" process — where plates could be prepared in advance and could also record fast-moving images — simplified photography greatly.

Darkrooms weren't really dark: they had windows of yellow glass because early plates could not record yellow light.

CINEMA

Moving pictures will never catch on!

The movies started with a bet. A wealthy Californian racehorse owner wagered that horses took all their feet off the ground when they galloped. English photographer Eadweard Muybridge believed he could prove it. Though hot-headed and odd, Muybridge was as good as his word. He photographed a galloping horse not just once, but many times, creating the picture sequences which would become movies.

Muybridge later captured other animals, and people, in his photographic sequences.

Moving animals

To create his sequence photographs, Muybridge rigged up twelve cameras. Trip-wires triggered them as a horse passed by. A projector he built in 1879 made them move on a screen. Muybridge had almost invented movies — but they ran for only a second before repeating.

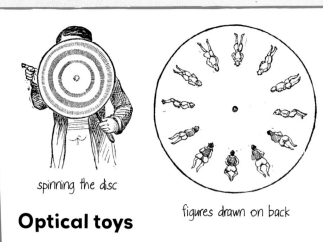

spinning the disc

figures drawn on back

Optical toys

Novelties that made drawings move were popular long before the movies. Gazing at a mirror through the slots of the spinning phenakistoscope disc made the figures drawn on the back dance realistically.

Peep-show parlour

Muybridge showed his picture sequences to Thomas Edison (see page 11) in 1886. Edison asked his assistant William Dickson to devise machines that would photograph and display longer sequences. It took five years, but the kinetoscope the pair built caused a sensation. A long strip of film snaked through this battery-powered box. Dropping a coin in the slot set the film in motion. When viewers peered through a peep-hole on the top, the rapidly-changing pictures moved realistically — for just 20 seconds! People queued to watch these coin-operated "peep-shows".

Movie murder

When Eadweard Muybridge's wife received a love-letter from another man, Muybridge called at his house. Announcing, "... here is the answer to the letter you sent my wife..." he shot the lover dead. Muybridge was tried for murder, but the court decided he had acted reasonably.

Edison and Co.

Thomas Edison was without doubt an inventive American genius. However, he ran a huge and busy research laboratory, and relied heavily on the work of others. Though Edison took the credit for his movie camera and viewer, much of the work was done by his British assistant William Dickson.

Thomas Alva Edison
1847–1931

William Kennedy Dickson
1860–1935

RECORDED SOUND

A musical box might be charming — but how many times would you listen to the same tune? Yet until 1877 machines like these were the only way of playing back music. True sound recording began with the phonograph: a toy that embossed wiggling lines of sound on a tin tube. Its inventor Thomas Edison (see page 11) said it was worthless. Others called it a "crude fake". Sound recordings weren't successful until they could be stamped out on a plastic disc by the thousand.

Organ grinding

Early 19th-century music machines like the musical box all relied on a slowly-turning cylinder to store their melodies. Pins fixed in its surface twanged the teeth of a tuneful metal comb in the musical box. In the bigger barrel organ, they opened valves that blew air into tiny organ pipes. More expensive models came with extra cylinders so that you could change the tune, but the choice of music was still very limited!

Street musicians called organ grinders cranked barrel organs, sending tame squirrel monkeys round to collect change.

The original disc jockey

Eleven years after Edison launched his phonograph, German-American inventor Emile Berliner found a way to record sound on flat discs. Using a simple press, he could then make countless identical copies of the original. Like Edison's tubes, the disc players were toys until famous musicians began making and selling recordings. Berliner's method of recording survived basically unchanged until the compact disc replaced it nearly a century later.

Berliner discs made the parties of the 1890s really rock.

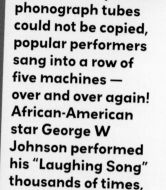

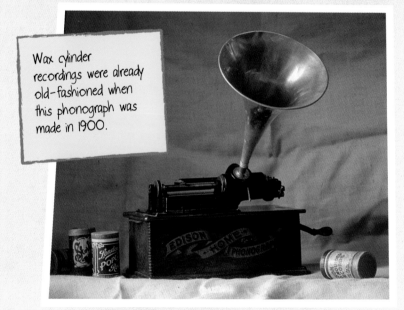

Wax cylinder recordings were already old-fashioned when this phonograph was made in 1900.

Sound on a cylinder

Edison soon replaced the tinfoil of his phonograph recordings with hard wax tubes. These wore out after playing them about 20 times, but then phonograph owners could recycle them. With the aid of a recording attachment, they could shave off the worn-out music grooves, and record their own performances.

MASS PRODUCTION

When the brakes on your bike wear down, you can be sure that the new pair you buy will fit, for every bike part is a standard size and shape. Each was made using machines that turn out identical parts, over and over again. It seems like common sense, yet two centuries ago nothing fitted neatly together like this.

Handmade confusion

Parts of 18th-century machines were like leaves on a tree: though they looked similar, they were never identical. Craftsmen made everything with hand tools like drills and files. Every part got individual attention, so making anything was costly and slow. Problems didn't end in the factory. When a part broke, you couldn't just swap it for another: a craftsman had to repair the whole machine.

Two soldiers who broke different parts of their weapons could not assemble one working gun from the good parts of each.

Interchangeable heaven

French inventor Honoré Blanc astonished politicians and generals in 1790. Picking parts of a gun from a box that contained dozens, he fitted together a working weapon. By carefully measuring parts as they were made, Blanc had made each one a standard size. Blanc's achievement was forgotten in France, but in the United States, inventor Eli Whitney used it to make guns for the army. His methods became known as the "American system of manufacture".

sheave — shell

iron pin

Machines to make machines

Each ship in Britain's Royal Navy needed hundreds of blocks: wheels that ropes ran round, inside wooden casings. In 1808 Marc Isambard Brunel – father of Isambard Kingdom Brunel (see page 9) – invented machines to make blocks.

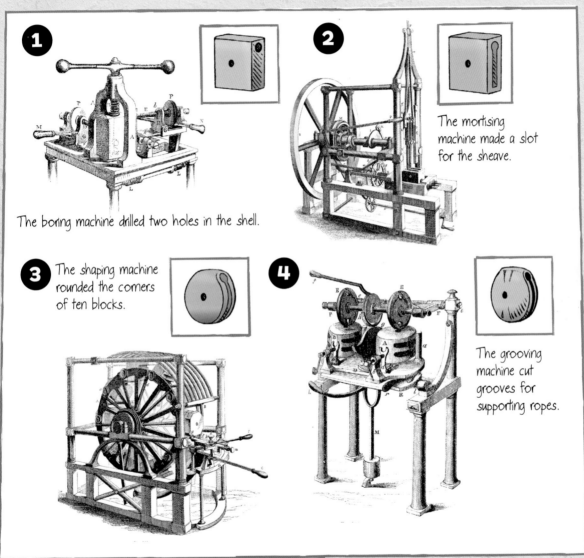

1 The boring machine drilled two holes in the shell.

2 The mortising machine made a slot for the sheave.

3 The shaping machine rounded the corners of ten blocks.

4 The grooving machine cut grooves for supporting ropes.

First off the block

It took 110 highly-skilled craftsmen to make the 130,000 blocks the British navy needed each year. Using machines invented by Brunel, ten unskilled men could do the job.

MACHINE GUN

Everyone knows that warfare is grim, bloody and deadly. But 19th-century engineers believed that war was inefficient, too. Enemy soldiers obstinately refused to die, however many times they were shot at, or slashed with razor-sharp swords. So ingenious inventors searched keenly for better, faster, more murderous ways of fighting.

Nineteenth-century battles were not as glorious and brave as this idealised picture suggests.

Swords and muskets

A battlefield was a terrifying place of confusion and danger. Cavalry (horse-riding soldiers) charged at the enemy, slashing with long swords. Foot soldiers were armed with muskets, but these were not accurate beyond 90 m (100 yd) and after each shot they took half a minute to load with gunpowder and musket ball.

Tit-for-rat-a-tat-tat

Cartridges, invented in the mid-19th century, fixed gunpowder and ball together in a metal tube. They allowed soldiers to load and fire far more quickly, but still not quickly enough. Inventors built rapid-firing guns from 1860, but none was as successful as Hiram Maxim's 1884 machine gun.

The cartridges themselves powered Maxim's gun. As well as propelling a bullet forward, each small blast ejected the empty cartridge case, and loaded a fresh one. A single Maxim gun could fire ten bullets a second.

Maxim's gun could be mounted on a two-wheeled carriage like a field gun, to make it portable.

Trench warfare

Maxim's gun, and other inventions such as barbed wire, changed warfare. Charging an enemy equipped with machine guns led to mass slaughter. By the time of the First World War (1914–18) battlefields became seas of mud, criss-crossed with trenches where troops (right) sheltered while bullets flew overhead.

WIRELESS TELEGRAPHY

Have you ever dreamed of inventing something that will change the world? The 20-year-old Italian student, Guglielmo Marconi, did just that. The "wireless telegraphy" system he devised allowed ships far out at sea to communicate for the first time. Today Marconi's brilliant idea powers everything from sat-nav to bus passes. We call it "radio".

Out of touch

The Morse telegraph (see page 13) brought land communication into the electric age, but this didn't help sailors or passengers on ships at sea. Once they had sailed out of sight of land, they were out of touch until they reached their destination. For signalling over short distances, they relied on a system that had been in use for 2,000 years: flags.

Each brightly coloured flag stood for a letter. Signallers looked in a code book to find three-letter codes for common words or phrases.

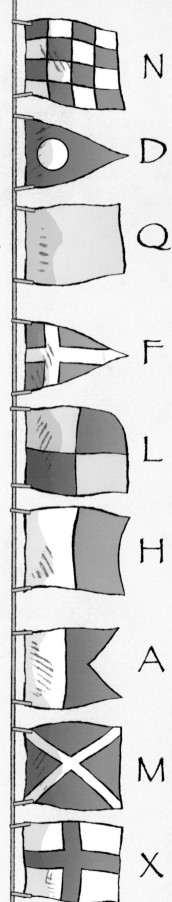

N
D
Q
F
L
H
A
M
X

Decoded, the message on the right reads:

NDQ = sharks
FLH = have eaten, or are eating
AMX = the Admiral

24

Marconi with some of the equipment he used in his wireless experiments.

Wireless magic

Studying electricity in 1894, Marconi became interested in "Hertzian waves": pulses of electrical power that travelled without wires. When he created the waves with sparks from a "transmitter", electricity flowed briefly through a "receiver" — powdered metal within a glass tube — on the other side of his attic workshop. The trick worked even when the receiver was at the end of his garden. Finally his brother carried the receiver over a hill. When he heard its crackling signals he alerted Guglielmo by firing a rifle.

Shipwreck radio

When he got no support in Italy, Marconi moved to Britain to develop "wireless telegraphy". By 1901, he succeeded in sending a message across the Atlantic. Ships began to fit wireless apparatus from 1899. One of the biggest, *Titanic*, showed the value of Marconi's invention when she struck an iceberg in 1912. Radio distress signals brought rescuers to the sinking ship, saving more than 700 lives.

25

It's all about poo!

MOTOR CAR

Today, cars are killing our world. The polluting carbon dioxide they produce is warming the Earth's climate. Our grandchildren may live in fiery, parched deserts. So you might be surprised to learn that when motor cars were invented at the end of the 19th century, they were welcomed as a way of **ending** pollution...

Dirty, smelly, polluting ... HORSES?

Land transport for most of the 19th century meant just one thing: a horse. To pull cabs and buses alone, London had 50,000 of them. Each produced 7-15 kg (15-35 lb) of poo a day. Horse transport was growing so fast that it was estimated that by 1950 London streets would be nearly 3 m (9 ft) deep in dung. Something had to be done!

Pongy pollution

New York street sweepers removed more than a thousand tons of horse dung each night.

The rattle of iron-clad wheels and horse shoes made busy streets noisy places.

Seemed like a good idea…

"Horseless carriages" promised to clear the streets of animals and their waste. Steam cars developed from much bigger "traction" engines around 1873. Electric motors powered many horseless carriages from the 1880s. But it was the invention of the internal combustion engine in 1862 that helped motor cars take over city streets. The change was swift. In 1903 London had only one motor cab, and 11,000 horse cabs. Ten years later there were 8,000 motor cabs and only 1,900 horse cabs.

Too fast!

Until 1896 British motor cars were not permitted to drive faster than 3 kph (2 mph). They had to have a crew of three, one of whom walked 60 paces ahead waving a red flag to warn of the "locomotive's" approach.

Honk! Honk!

Many opposed motor cars because they feared the vehicles would terrify horses, causing accidents.

Fire inside

"Internal combustion" is just a grand way to say "fire inside". A petrol engine's fuel burns inside the cylinder that powers it, not outside, as on a steam engine. Valves at the cylinder's end let in a fuel-air mixture (1) which the piston squeezes tight (2). A spark makes the fuel burn (3) driving back the piston, which finally forces out the waste gases (4).

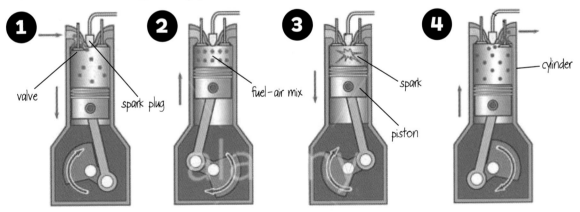

1 — valve, spark plug
2 — fuel-air mix
3 — spark, piston
4 — cylinder

TUNNELLING

What's more interesting than boring? To Marc Isambard Brunel, boring was the most interesting thing in the world! This 19th-century engineer (see page 21) pioneered a way of boring tunnels through soft, wet ground. His invention made possible modern road and rail links that pass under rivers, and burrow deep below cities.

Engineers can bore for England!

Mud and flood

Tunnelling through rock is an ancient art. It is possible using only picks and shovels, but explosives — particularly dynamite, invented in 1860 — made tunnelling faster and easier. Digging a tunnel through soft ground, though, was a different matter. Even when heavy timber propped up the roof, there was always the danger of striking a hidden stream that would flood the tunnel.

Early 19th-century cartoonists had fun imagining what would happen to people who dared to enter a tunnel under a river.

Pumping out

When one of his tunnels struck wet sand in 1835, British engineer George Stephenson tried to pump out the water. Thirteen pumps worked for a year and a half before tunnelling could continue.

Screw jacks pushed the shield forward into the mud as the tunnel grew in length.

Old but good

Brunel's tunnel lasted very well. It's still in use as part of London's rail transport network.

Bring me my shield!

In 1823 Marc Brunel had a brilliant idea. He wanted to cut a tunnel through soft mud under London's River Thames. So he built a "shield": 36 cast iron boxes, each big enough for a man with a shovel, and a bricklayer. Boards at the front of each box stopped mud flowing in. The shoveller took out one board at a time, and dug out a little mud to advance the tunnel. The bricklayer behind him built a waterproof lining as the tunnel moved forward.

Compressed air

Though Brunel's shield protected the tunnellers, floods nevertheless killed several of them. The problem of flooding was eventually solved by pumping air into tunnels under construction. The air pushed back against the wet mud, keeping the tunnel dry.

GLOSSARY

barge Cargo ship, often without an engine, towed by an animal or another ship.

bet Competition in which people who wrongly guess how an unpredictable event will end pay money to those who guess correctly.

blocks Arrangement of wheels through which ropes pass, to change their direction or increase their pulling power.

cab Taxi.

canal Artificial river dug to carry ships or to channel water.

canvas Piece of fabric stretched on a frame, on which an artist paints a picture.

carbon dioxide Gas that mixes naturally with other gases in the air, but which causes climate change when increased by burning coal and oil.

cargo Load carried by a vehicle, especially a ship.

cast iron Form of iron metal that creates complex shapes when melted and moulded.

climate Pattern of weather at a place, recorded over many years.

code Way of storing information so that it can be transmitted more quickly and efficiently, or in a form that machines can read and understand.

compact disc Small silvery disc used to store music in computer code.

dung Solid waste dropped from an animal's gut.

dynamo Device that turns movement into electricity.

emboss To press a pattern into a surface.

facility Freedom from difficulty.

filament Slender thread.

freight Transport of goods, especially by sea.

guinea Old fashioned sum of money equal to £1.05.

hold Storage space low down in the ship.

hull Body of a ship or boat that floats in the water.

liner Large, often luxurious ocean ship built to carry passengers.

locomotive Engine on wheels that can move itself and pull a load along rails.

mph Miles per hour.

musket Old-fashioned gun with a long barrel, fired from the shoulder like a rifle.

passenger liner See LINER.

piston Metal block that slides to-and-fro inside an engine, driven by steam pressure or burning fuel.

plate (photographic) Sheet of glass covered in a light-sensitive layer, used in a camera to take photographs.

projector Device that lights up and magnifies a picture, so that it is enlarged on a screen.

propeller Arrangement of several slanting blades that spins on a ship or aircraft to power the vehicle forward.

receiver (telegraph) Device that receives or records a communications signal sent out by a TRANSMITTER.

resort Town, usually by the sea, visited by holiday-makers for health or relaxation.

sat-nav Device for guiding travellers using signals from a space-craft.

semaphore Communication method that sends signals using moving flaps or arms.

sequence Several numbers, letters, objects or signs arranged in a special order.

sheave Grooved wheel or pulley.

telegraph Communication device that sent either visible messages, using flapping arms, or electrical messages, using a code of pulses.

timber Wood used for construction.

translator Someone who converts spoken or written messages from one language to another.

transmitter Device that sends out a communication signal.

trip-wire A hidden wire laid at ankle height to catch the feet of a enemy, perhaps to trigger an explosion.

valve Device that allows a flow in one direction only.

wager *See* BET.

WEBSITES

SS *Great Britain*
http://www.ssgreatbritain.org/ShipsVoyages.aspx

Telegraph
http://www.sil.si.edu/Exhibitions/Underwater-Web/index.htm

Edison's light bulb
http://americanhistory.si.edu/lighting/19thcent/hall19.htm

Edison — cinema and sound recording
http://lcweb2.loc.gov/ammem/edhtml/edhome.html

Build a tunnel
http://www.pbs.org/wgbh/building-big/tunnel/challenge/index.html

Note to parents and teachers:
Every effort has been made by the Publishers to ensure that the websites in this book are suitable for children, that they are of the highest educational value, and that they contain no inappropriate or offensive material. However, because of the nature of the Internet, it is impossible to guarantee that the contents of these sites will not be altered. We strongly advise that Internet access is supervised by a responsible adult.

INDEX